Volume One, Issue Four

ON
THE CHRISTIAN LIFE

Fred Sanders

InterVarsity Press
Downers Grove, Illinois

©1999 by Fred R. Sanders
All rights reserved. No part of this book may be reproduced in any form without written permission from InterVarsity Press.

InterVarsity Press® is the book-publishing division of InterVarsity Christian Fellowship/USA®, a student movement active on campus at hundreds of universities, colleges and schools of nursing in the United States of America, and a member movement of the International Fellowship of Evangelical Students. For information about local and regional activities, write Public Relations Dept., InterVarsity Christian Fellowship/USA, 6400 Schroeder Rd., P.O. Box 7895, Madison, WI 53707-7895.

In most cases Scripture quotations are taken from the *New Revised Standard Version* of the Bible, copyright 1989 by the Division of Christian Education of the National Council of the Churches of Christ in the USA. Used by permission. All rights reserved.

ISBN 0-8308-2244-5

Printed in the United States of America ∞

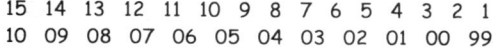

15 14 13 12 11 10 9   8   7   6   5   4   3   2   1
10 09 08 07 06 05 04 03 02 01 00 99

InterVarsity Press
P.O. Box 1400
Downers Grove, IL 60515

World Wide Web: www.ivpress.com

E-mail: mail@ivpress.com

CONTENTS

INTRODUCTION..................4

Phun with Ephesians...........7
MEET PAUL..........................16

Sin Safari..................17
MEET PAUL TILLICH................36

The Vine..................37
MEET JOHN WESLEY.................46

THEO & DEMPFEY'S WORD PAGE......47
THE MEADOW........................48

Blessed be the God and Father of our Lord Jesus Christ, who has blessed us in Christ with every spiritual blessing in the heavenly places, just as he chose us in Christ before the foundation of the world to be holy and blameless before him in love.

He destined us for adoption as his children through Jesus Christ, according to the good pleasure of his will, to the praise of his glorious grace that he freely bestowed on us in the Beloved.

In him we have redemption through his blood, the forgiveness of our trespasses, according to the riches of his grace that he lavished on us.

With all wisdom and insight he has made known to us the mystery of his will, according to his good pleasure that he set forth in Christ, as a plan for the fullness of time, to gather up all things in him, things in heaven and things on earth.

In Christ we have also obtained an inheritance, having been destined according to the purpose of him who accomplishes all things according to his counsel and will, so that we, who were the first to set our hope on Christ, might live for the praise of his glory.

NOW WE CERTAINLY *GAIN* SOMETHING FROM THIS. *INHERITANCE* IS THE WORD THIS TRANSLATION USES. NOW AND FOREVER OUR LIVES ARE TRANSFORMED, ENRICHED AND DEEPENED AS WE TAKE OUR PART IN WHAT GOD IS DOING IN CHRIST!

SCHWARTZ! WHERE'D YA *GO?* I CAN'T SEE YA!

HEH HEH!

BUT WHAT'S IN IT FOR *US* ISN'T THE *MAIN* THING! OUR LIVES ARE TAKEN UP INTO GOD'S OVERALL PLAN, AND WE BECOME *LIVING PRAISE*, SO THAT THE *MEANING* OF OUR LIVES IS--HERE'S THAT PHRASE AGAIN-- THE *PRAISE OF GOD'S GLORY!*

SCHWARTZY! HEY, *SCHWARTZ!* WHERE *ARE* YA?

NOW--THIS IS IMPORTANT--OUR SALVATION AND OUR PLACE IN THIS WHOLE *MOVEMENT* OF GOD'S PLAN FOR THE WORLD IN CHRIST ISN'T *COMPLETE* UNTIL WE RECEIVE THE *HOLY SPIRIT*, WHO *CONSECRATES* US AS PEOPLE WHO BELONG TO GOD. THE SPIRIT FLOWS OUT

HEY! IS THAT THAT *BELLY-WATER* YOU WAS TALKIN' ABOUT?

YES! YES, DEMPFEY, THE *SPIRIT* IS THE *BELLY-WATER!* FOR PITY'S SAKE, WILL YOU QUIT *HOUNDING* ME ABOUT THE BELLY-WATER LONG ENOUGH FOR ME TO *FINISH* COMMENTING ON THIS PASSAGE?!!

GOSH! NO NEED TO LOSE YOUR *SANCTIFICATION* OVER IT! I WAS JUST *ASKIN'*!

In him you also, when you had heard the word of truth, the gospel of your salvation, and had believed in him, were marked with the seal of the promised Holy Spirit; this is the pledge of our inheritance toward redemption as God's own people, to the praise of his glory.

MEET THE THEOLOGIANS

THE APOSTLE PAUL

PAUL'S LIFE AND TRAVELS ARE DESCRIBED IN TWO PLACES IN THE BIBLE: THE BOOK OF ACTS AND THE BOOK OF MAPS (FOUND IN THE VERY BACK). HE WAS TIRELESS IN HIS DESIRE TO SPREAD THE GOSPEL, AND HE WORE OUT PLENTY OF SHOES, SHIPS AND ASSISTANTS ALONG THE WAY.

PAUL, WITH HIS CAREFUL RABBINIC TRAINING, WAS PROBABLY THE MOST THOROUGH THINKER AMONG THE APOSTLES! HE SAW THE IMPLICATIONS THAT THE CHRISTIAN MESSAGE HAD FOR THE ENTIRE WORLD SOONER AND MORE CLEARLY THAN ANYONE ELSE DID! AND HE WROTE IT DOWN!

A LOT OF PEOPLE THINK THAT PAUL'S CENTRAL IDEA AND FAVORITE TOPIC WAS JUSTIFICATION BY FAITH, BECAUSE HE WROTE SO MUCH ABOUT IT AND DEFENDED IT WITH SO MUCH ENERGY AND PASSION. BUT PROBABLY HE ONLY WROTE SO MUCH ABOUT IT BECAUSE HE KEPT BEING MISUNDERSTOOD BY PEOPLE WHO JUST NEVER QUITE GOT THE IDEA. SO HE KEPT GOING BACK TO SQUARE ONE AND TRYING TO POUND IT INTO PEOPLE'S HEADS, NO MATTER HOW LONG IT TOOK...

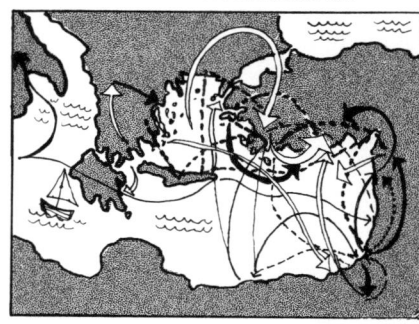

"I'M IN HERE!"
"YOU'RE IN HERE!"
"SO'S THE WORLD!"
"AND GOD!"

"OH, *I GET IT*! 'JUSTIFICATION' MEANS, 'JUST IF I CAN BE *GOOD* ENOUGH, GOD WILL ACCEPT ME,' RIGHT?"

"GIVE ME STRENGTH!"

IN FACT, THE CENTRAL IDEA THAT REALLY SEEMED TO GRIP PAUL'S IMAGINATION WAS MORE LIKELY THE IDEA OF BEING "IN CHRIST." ANYONE WHO IS IN CHRIST IS A NEW CREATION, BECAUSE GOD WAS IN CHRIST RECONCILING THE WORLD TO HIMSELF. PARTICIPATION IN CHRIST'S SUFFERINGS AND RESURRECTION IS AT THE CENTER OF EVERYTHING PAUL HAS TO SAY ABOUT CHRISTIANITY.

ANOTHER IMPORTANT THING TO LOOK FOR IN HIS WRITINGS IS HIS CONVICTION THAT THE COMING OF JESUS AS THE MESSIAH IS THE END OF THE WORLD AS WE KNOW IT. THE OLD ORDER OF THE WORLD HAS PASSED AWAY, AND CHRIST HAS BROUGHT THE REALITY OF GOD'S KINGDOM INTO OUR MIDST. NOW OF COURSE PAUL WAS REALISTIC ABOUT THE SORRY STATE THAT THE WORLD CONTINUES TO BE IN, BUT HE WAS SERIOUS ABOUT THE FACT THAT WE HAVE PASSED FROM THE KINGDOM OF DARKNESS INTO THE KINGDOM OF LIGHT.

PAUL'S MOST COMPREHENSIVE PRESENTATION OF THE GOSPEL IS FOUND IN ROMANS BECAUSE IN THAT BOOK HE REALLY STARTS OUT WITH FIRST PRINCIPLES AND THEN BUILDS ON THEM. BUT THE BOOK OF EPHESIANS IS ALSO AN EXCELLENT SUMMARY OF PAUL'S THEOLOGY BECAUSE IT PRESENTS SUCH A BROAD VIEW OF THE UNIVERSAL SIGNIFICANCE OF JESUS CHRIST. JUST IMAGINE: PAUL HAD NO IDEA HE WAS WRITING THE BIBLE; HE WAS JUST DOING HIS BEST TO DESCRIBE WHAT THE LORD HAS DONE.

"I HAVE BEEN CRUCIFIED WITH CHRIST; AND IT IS NO LONGER I WHO LIVE, BUT IT IS CHRIST WHO LIVES IN ME. AND THE LIFE I NOW LIVE IN THE FLESH I LIVE BY FAITH IN THE SON OF GOD, WHO LOVED ME AND GAVE HIMSELF FOR ME!"

SIN SAFARI

As the sun slowly sets and the sky's getting starry,
Prepare to embark on the Great Sin Safari!
I'll be your guide on this bold expedition
Straight to the heart of the human condition.
We'll see lots of sins in their own native setting;
Take photos, but PLEASE! --no feeding or petting.
With so many kinds of sin under the sun,
It seems like we've each got our own favorite one.
Some are exotic and some are mundane;
Some make you neurotic! Some drive you insane!
But we don't have to go far or search very hard;
Why, most of it's right here in our own backyard!
So follow me, kids, gentle women and men:
The Great Sin Safari's about to begin!

The first thing we find is this cramped crowd of critters:
They're Jitter-Me-Bugs, and they all have the jitters.
From sun-up to sun-down the whole darn society
Is driven by dread, worry, fear and anxiety.
Their past is a fright and their future is fearful,
Ask, "What are you scared of?" and you'll get an ear-full:
They worry 'bout houses and spouses and jobs,
And food, drink and fashion, and thing-a-ma-bobs.

They worry 'bout black holes and quasars and pulsars;
They worry they're giving their stomachs big ulcers!
They worry their friends will find out they're a fraud;
The pious ones worry they're not trusting God!
Some cover their fear by behaving unruly,
And *there's* one who hides it by being a bully!
But all of them jitter, and so I'm not sorry
To turn the next page in the Great Sin Safari!

Next we encounter a sin who's a winner,
A web-weaving bug called the Googol-pod Spinner.
He's busy full-time and won't take a vacation;
He's fully engaged in: Self-Justification!
He does what he pleases, then stays up all night
Spinning webs out of words to convince him he's right.
He talks in a circle with arguments tricky
And rationalizes until the web's sticky;

And once it's all sticky, he waits till he catches
A scapegoat or two! Oh, the miserable wretches!
He names them and blames them and passes the buck,
And explains that he's only involved through bad luck.
His millions of fingers direct your attention
Away from his crimes, which he hopes you won't mention.
He's learned the great lesson that's sweeping the nation:
It's better to give than receive condemnation.

What's next on the Great Sin Safari, you wonder?
The Tempt-O-Guilt Monster, whose voice is like thunder!
...Or is his voice gentle, and smooth and inviting?
Or both? I'm not sure, I have trouble deciding.
For as you can see, this on-his-back-lay-er
Is a two-headed, twin-bedded, spiteful game-player!
His idea of fun is to keep someone busy
Just running in circles until they get dizzy.
His belly's a racetrack for rats to run races
Between the extremes of his two ghastly faces.

One head is temptation, to beguile and entice you;
The other is guilt, to condemn, slice and dice you.
First he will offer a vice that's attractive,
Then play on your conscience 'til it's hyperactive.
That's what he likes most: Just keeping you running
With his "Why don't you try it?"
         and "Look what you've done!"-ing.
"You're a sinner," he says, "So you might as well sin,
And keep running around in this rut that you're in!"
Look out! Once you're trapped by his double-bind curse
You're not even free to run 'round in reverse.

T he Gitter's a critter who knows what he's after:
He's stockpiled his fortress from basement to rafter
With all kinds of money and food and commodities,
And knick-knacks and items and objects and oddities.

He's not much for talking,
His voice is all raspy,
His ten thousand fingers are constantly graspy.
He's laying up treasures from sunup to sundown;
It keeps him so busy that he's always rundown.
The whole world's a stage, and he's sure of his role:
Possession, it seems, is nine-tenths of his soul.
He's sure his life's meaning consists of this stuff,
Which is why there's no way he can gather enough.
It's hard to believe, as he lays there all curled,
That this is the varmint who runs the whole world.

On the whole Sin Safari, there's no sin that's finer
Than the sin that is known as the I-Me-My-Miner.
Well, at least he's his OWN favorite, that much is clear.
There is no one and nothing that he holds so dear
As his OWN self, his OWN life, his OWN point of view;
He can't find the time for me or for you.
Now don't be alarmed, and don't get your spine chilled,
But we've just stumbled into his I-me-my-minefield!
It's a place where you'll find, if you happen to enter,
That all roads converge on the Me at the center.
And that Me is Him: He's Priority One,
And he's proud of his life and of all that he's done.
He's proud and he'll shout it, he's not prone to mumble:
He's proud that he's clever and proud that he's humble.
He's proud that he's neat, with each thing in its place,
And his place is the center! The whole human race
Is a means to an end for his gratification;
The whole universe is his self-service station.
When he's on the throne, he feels totally tidy,
Surrounded by you, me, and good God Almighty.
That's the I-Me-My-Miner. Do I hear you snoring?
I can't really blame you; this critter is boring.

She has no opinions or thoughts or concerns,
And nothing to offer the world as it turns.
She isn't self-centered! Good grief, don't be silly!
In fact, she's not centered on ANYTHING, really!
God made her for something, but maybe she's stalling;
Politely declining to rise to her calling.
Of all the poor sins she just might be the poorest,
She's blending right in with the trees in her forest.
I'd sure like to meet her; I'm sure that she's pleasant.
But I'm not sure I see her. Is she really present?

Now everyone knows about sin, sins and sinning:
Sin's been the whole problem right from the beginning.
But really to know all sin's horror and FEEL it...
To do that, you have to let Jesus reveal it.
Knowledge of sin isn't some kind of "given";
We learn what sin is when we learn we're forgiven.

We're so out of whack and we're so far off track,
We don't know how lost we were, 'til we get back!
We've fallen a long way, not just kind of sort of;
It's the glory of God that we've all fallen short of.
Our sin is for real—it's not some fancy fiction;
The problem's so bad it required crucifixion.

On this swell safari we've seen all these varmints
In native surroundings, in typical garments.
This is where they belong, out of doors in the wild,
So don't try to make one a pet for your child.
You can't take them home or nickname them "Rover;"
If you keep them around, they will always take over.
Though you'll find it in houses all over the nation,
Sin doesn't respond well to domestication.
The problem is one of which I haven't spoken,
But here it is: Sin simply can't be housebroken.
It would rather break houses. It will, if you let it:
It's an expert homewrecker, and don't you forget it.

Well, we're all out of time for this bold expedition,
Through sins of great malice and sins of omission.
If I left out your favorite, forgive me! I'm sorry!
But this is the end of the Great Sin Safari!

MEET THE THEOLOGIANS

PAUL TILLICH

PAUL TILLICH WAS ONE OF THE MOST INFLUENTIAL THEOLOGIANS OF THE TWENTIETH CENTURY. HE SAW HIMSELF AS CARRYING ON THE GREAT TASK OF APOLOGETICS: EXPLAINING AND DEFENDING THE CHRISTIAN FAITH TO THE OUTSIDE WORLD. HE ALWAYS WROTE WITH THE SKEPTICS IN MIND.

TILLICH WAS A MILITARY CHAPLAIN DURING WORLD WAR I IN HIS NATIVE GERMANY; HE SAW THE HORRORS OF WAR UP CLOSE AND PERSONAL. AFTER THE WAR, HE BECAME A THEOLOGY PROFESSOR. BUT HE WAS AN OUTSPOKEN CRITIC OF THE NAZIS, AND WHEN THEY CAME TO POWER IN 1933, TILLICH WAS OUT OF A JOB. HE CAME TO AMERICA, WHERE HE TAUGHT THEOLOGY UNTIL HIS DEATH IN 1965. SO AMERICA'S MOST FAMOUS MODERN THEOLOGIAN... WAS REALLY GERMAN. OH WELL.

TILLICH BELIEVED THAT HIS JOB AS A THEOLOGIAN WAS TO LISTEN CLOSELY TO THE QUESTIONS THAT PEOPLE ARE ASKING IN THEIR DAILY LIVES. HE WANTED TO KNOW WHAT THEIR DEEPEST, MOST SERIOUS, ULTIMATE CONCERNS WERE. AND THEN HE COULD BRING OUT THE RESOURCES OF THE GOSPEL TO MEET THOSE NEEDS THAT HE SAW EXPRESSED IN CONTEMPORARY SOCIETY. HE CALLED THIS THE METHOD OF CORRELATION: LINKING UP IMPORTANT SECULAR QUESTIONS WITH THE APPROPRIATE THEOLOGICAL ANSWERS.

ONE EXAMPLE OF TILLICH'S USE OF THIS METHOD WAS HIS RE-INTERPRETATION OF SIN AND SALVATION. HE SHOWED THAT WHAT CHRISTIANS HAD ALWAYS CALLED "SIN" WAS THE SAME THING AS WHAT THE MODERN WORLD WAS CALLING "ESTRANGEMENT," AND "SALVATION" WAS A WAY OF TALKING ABOUT "RECONCILIATION." BY USING PSYCHOLOGICAL TERMS HE HELPED MANY PEOPLE SEE THE THEOLOGICAL MEANING OF THEIR OWN SITUATIONS.

TILLICH LOVED ART AND PHILOSOPHY. SOMETIMES HE COULD TALK IN A WAY THAT WOULD MAKE YOUR HEAD SPIN, ABOUT "THE GROUND OF BEING," "BEING ITSELF," "THE GOD ABOVE GOD" AND "ULTIMATE CONCERN." BUT HE COULD ALSO PROCLAIM THE GOSPEL IN DOWN-TO-EARTH TERMS THAT REACHED PEOPLE RIGHT WHERE THEY LIVED:

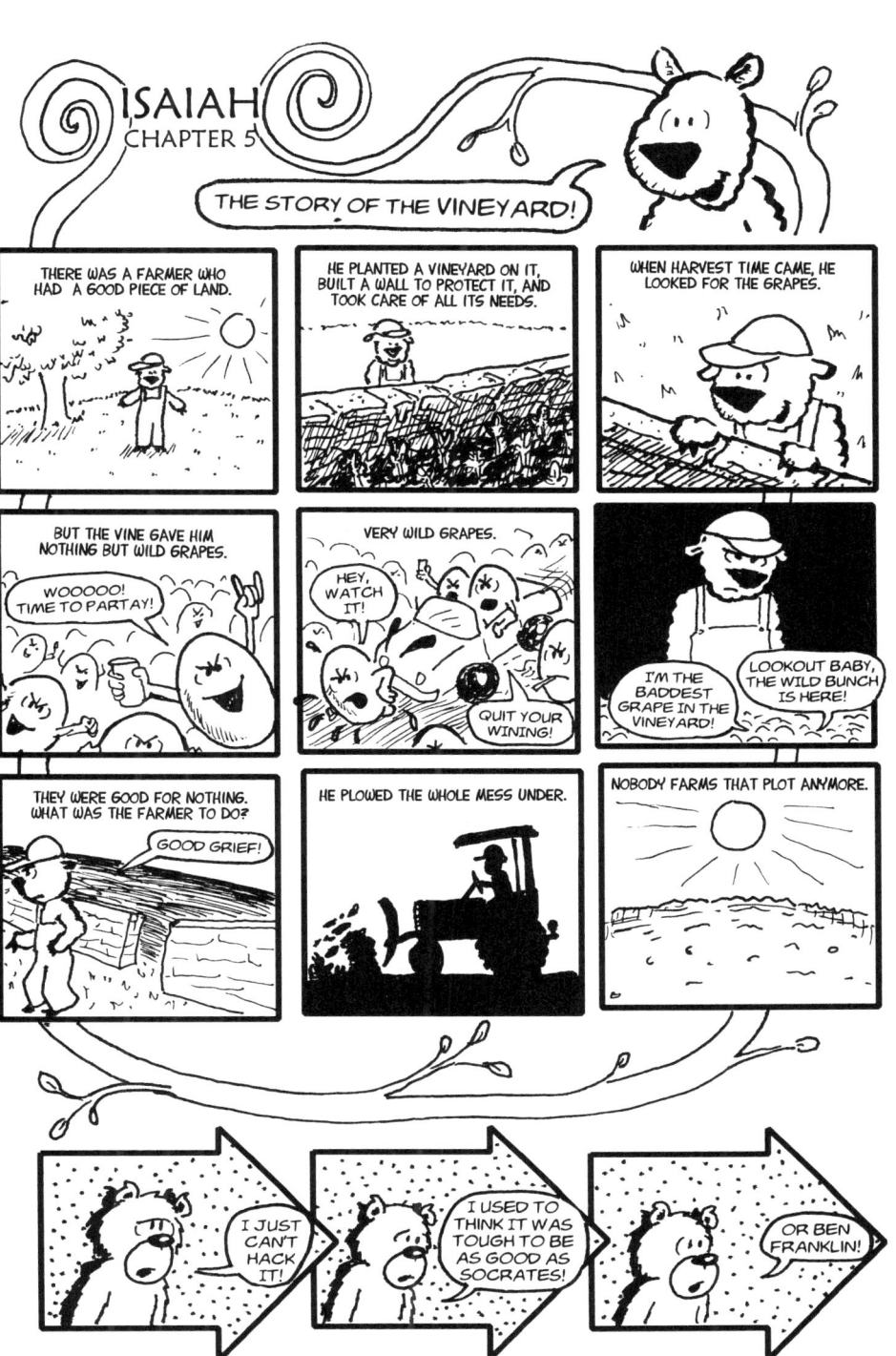

MEET THE THEOLOGIANS

John Wesley
1703 - 1791

JOHN WESLEY'S MINISTRY SHAPED A REVIVAL MOVEMENT THAT TRANSFORMED ENGLAND AND SWEPT THE WORLD. HIS EMPHASIS ON "HOLINESS OF HEART AND LIFE" HAS CAUGHT THE IMAGINATION OF ALL KINDS OF CHRISTIANS AND MADE HIM A CONTINUING INSPIRATION NOT JUST FOR METHODISTS BUT FOR THE ENTIRE CHURCH.

WESLEY CAME FROM A VERY LARGE AND DEVOUT FAMILY. HE LEARNED A LOT FROM HIS MOTHER, SUSANNA, AND HE WORKED CLOSELY WITH HIS BROTHER CHARLES WHO IS FAMOUS FOR HIS MANY HYMNS. WHEN JOHN WAS SEVEN YEARS OLD, HE WAS RESCUED FROM A HOUSE FIRE. HE LATER CONSIDERED HIS LIFE "A BRAND PLUCKED FROM THE BURNING," AND HE LIVED ON BORROWED TIME.

THROUGHOUT HIS EARLY TWENTIES, WESLEY GREW MORE AND MORE SERIOUS IN HIS CHRISTIAN LIFE AND COMMITMENT. FOR YEARS IT SEEMED THAT EVERY BOOK HE PICKED UP CHALLENGED HIM TO A DEEPER LIFE OF FAITH IN CHRIST. ALL OF THIS CAME TO A HEAD ON MAY 24, 1738, WHEN WESLEY'S HEART WAS "STRANGELY WARMED" BY ASSURANCE OF SALVATION IN CHRIST.

WESLEY'S TRADEMARK DOCTRINE WAS CHRISTIAN PERFECTION, ALSO CALLED ENTIRE SANCTIFICATION.

I... WILL... BE... GOOD!

*THERE'S **GOT** TO BE MORE TO LIFE THAN THIS...*

HE WANTED TO EMPHASIZE THE RENEWAL THAT JESUS COULD MAKE IN THE GROUND OF A PERSON'S HEART. THE NOTION OF DISCIPLESHIP AS A NEVER-ENDING FIGHT AGAINST YOUR OWN WICKED HEART DIDN'T SEEM LIKE A GOOD MODEL OF CHRISTIAN MATURITY TO RECOMMEND.

WESLEY MAINTAINED THAT JESUS CHRIST WAS ABLE TO SAVE "TO THE UTTERMOST" ALL THOSE WHO TRUST IN HIM, AND THIS MEANT THAT JESUS WANTED TO RULE ALONE IN OUR HEARTS, SUBDUING ALL THINGS TO HIMSELF. RESIGNING YOURSELF TO LIVE PERMANENTLY WITH SIN SEEMED TO HIM LIKE AN INSULT TO THE SAVIOR'S COMPETENCE, AND A DENIAL OF THE REAL PURPOSE OF CHRISTIAN LIFE:

WESLEY WAS AN EFFECTIVE PREACHER AND AN AMAZINGLY PRODUCTIVE PERSON. HE MADE THE MOST OF HIS COMMUTING TIME, RIDING ZILLIONS OF MILES ON HORSEBACK (THE REAL STATISTICS WOULD JUST MAKE YOU FEEL LAZY BY COMPARISON) WITH THE REINS IN ONE HAND AND A BOOK IN THE OTHER. HE SOMETIMES DESCRIBED HIMSELF AS "A MAN OF ONE BOOK," THE BIBLE. OF COURSE HE DIDN'T MEAN THAT LITERALLY! AFTER ALL, HE READ VERY WIDELY AND EVEN WROTE AND EDITED DOZENS OF BOOKS HIMSELF.

*LET THE SPIRIT RETURN TO **GOD** WHO **GAVE** IT, WITH THE WHOLE **TRAIN** OF ITS AFFECTIONS!*

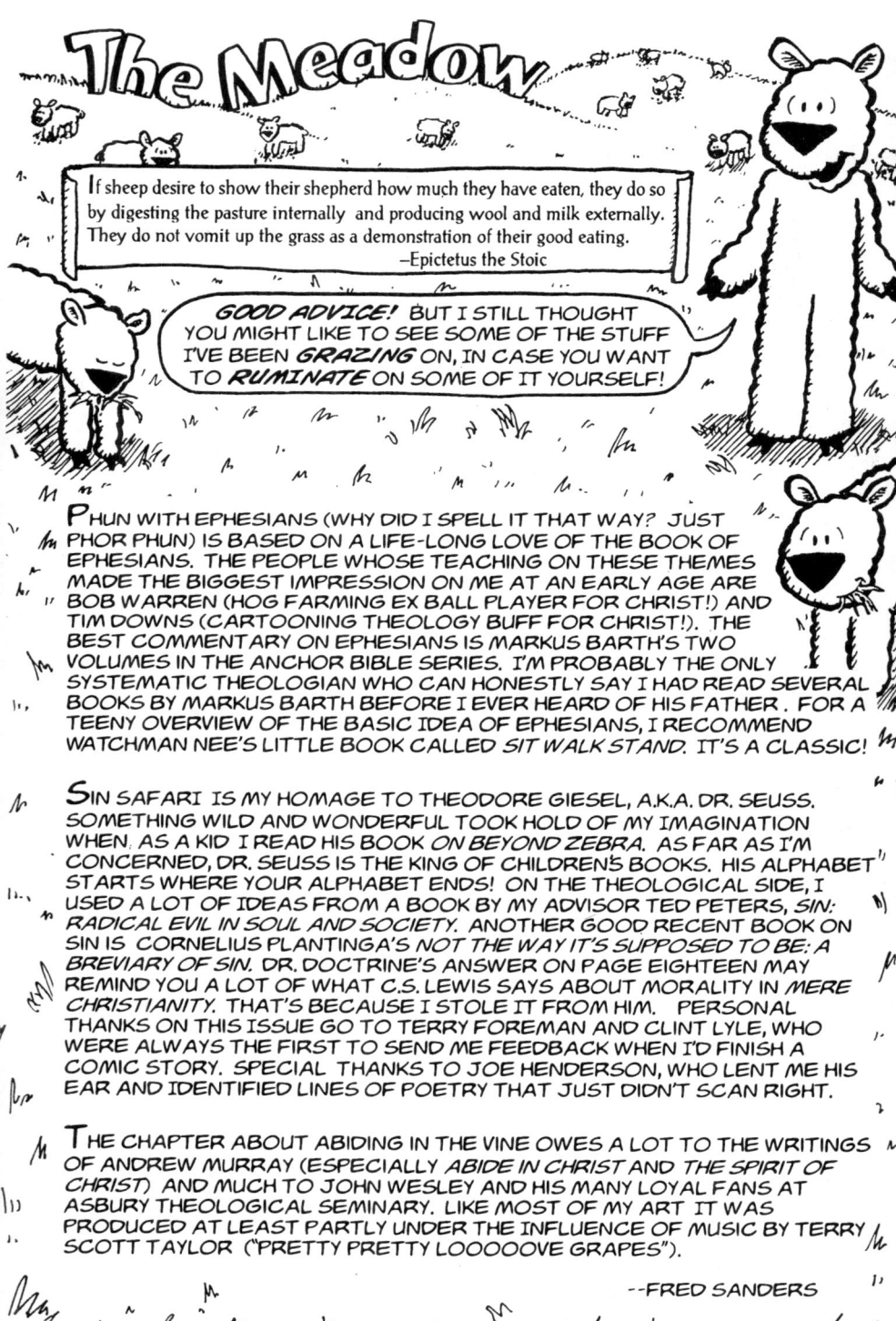